COMPUTER GAMES

NANCY DICKMANN

Published in 2024 by
KidHaven Publishing, an Imprint of Greenhaven Publishing, LLC
2544 Clinton St., Buffalo, NY 14224

Text and Editor: Nancy Dickmann
Children's Publisher: Anne O'Daly
Design Manager: Keith Davis
Designer and Illustrator: Supriya Sahai
Picture Manager: Sophie Mortimer

Picture Credits
Key: t=top, b=bottom, c=center, l=left, r=right
Interior: Interior: Alamy: zixia 17; iStock: Chaosamran Studio 10; Shutterstock: SFIO CRACHO 4, DC Studio 25, Frame Stock Footage 14, 29t, frantic00 6, Friends Stock 5, goostock 7, 28t, Gorodenkoff 24, G-Stock Studio 9, Insta Photos 27, Paceman 21, PicMy 13, Pictureguy 16, Pixel-Shot 12, Stu Porter 15, Roman Samborsky 18, Konstantin Savusia 19, sdecoret 20, Tzido Sun 8, Diego Thomazini 11, 29b, Vadym Stock 26, Tero Vesalinen 22, Tommy Lee Walken 23.

Cataloging-in-Publication Data

Names: Dickmann, Nancy.
Title: Computer games / Nancy Dickmann.
Description: Buffalo, New York: KidHaven Publishing, 2024. |
Series: Cool computing jobs | Includes glossary and index.
Identifiers: ISBN 9781534546530 (pbk.) | ISBN 9781534546547 (library bound) | ISBN 9781534546554 (ebook)
Subjects: LCSH: Computer games--Programming--Vocational guidance--Juvenile literature. |
Video games--Design--Juvenile literature.
Classification: LCC QA76.76.C672 D534 2024 | DDC 794.8'1536 --dc23

Manufactured in the United States of America

CPSIA compliance information: Batch #CW24KH: For further information contact Greenhaven Publishing LLC at 1-844-317-7404.

Please visit our website, www.greenhavenpublishing.com.
For a free color catalog of all our high-quality books, call toll free 1-844-317-7404 or fax 1-844-317-7405.

Find us on

CONTENTS

01

{ }

A WORLD OF GAMES

Do you like to play computer games? Which one is your favorite?

Computer games have been around for more than 50 years. The earliest were very simple. Now we have sweeping adventures with amazing graphics. Some games are realistic. Others take you to alien worlds! Computer games are one kind of video game.

Some games use virtual reality (VR) to make it feel like you're a part of the game.

A Growing Industry

Video games are more than just fun. They're big business! The top games earn more than blockbuster movies. It can take years for a game to go from an idea to a finished product. There are many different jobs involved. Maybe one day, one of them could be yours!

Minecraft is one of the top-selling video games of all time, with over 200 million copies sold.

People all over the world buy and play computer games.

GAMING PLATFORMS

People could only play video games in arcades in the past. Now you can play practically anywhere!

Mobile game apps are great for long trips.

Many people play games on tablets or smartphones. Once they download the game, they can play wherever they like. These games are often fairly simple. They don't need a lot of memory or power from your device. You control them by touching the screen.

Each brand of console has its own controllers. They have many buttons for different moves.

Many consoles let you plug in other devices, such as gaming chairs that vibrate to help bring the game to life.

Bigger and Better

Many people play games on a personal computer (PC) or gaming console. These games can be bigger and more complicated, with better graphics. Some games come on a disk. Others are downloaded directly onto the console or computer.

01

GAME PRODUCERS

It takes a team to make a computer game. Every team needs a leader!

A game producer might be the person who came up with the original idea for the game.

A game producer takes the lead. They think about who is likely to buy the game. What features will they want? They think of characters and stories for the game. What will make the game stand out? The producer also works with artists and programmers.

Making It Work

A game producer often manages the project from start to finish. They manage a team and set budgets and schedules. They make sure that the game is the best that it can possibly be. They have to work well with others to make this happen.

When a new game is launched, the producer will give presentations and interviews about it.

A game producer needs leadership and teamwork skills.

CREATING A WORLD

Some computer games take you to another world. How exactly are these worlds created?

Some concept artists draw or paint by hand. Others use computer drawing tools.

A concept artist makes the first sketches of what the game will look like. They think about the world it is set in. They think about the characters and the tone of the game. Will the game be dark and spooky or fast-paced and fun? The concept art needs to match.

From Idea to Reality

An environment artist turns the concept artist's work into a 3D landscape. They create the digital environment where the game will take place. It might be the wilderness or an alien city! A 3D modeling artist makes digital models of characters, weapons, and vehicles.

If an environment is very detailed, the game could lag on some computers.

Every object that a character uses has to be created by a 3D modeling artist.

DESIGNING AN EXPERIENCE

What kinds of games do you like to play? Would you change anything about them?

A gameplay designer can learn what works by watching other people play.

How a game plays is just as important as how it looks. A gameplay designer figures out how a game will work. What are the rules? What is the player's main goal? What powers do the characters have, and how can players access them? How do you score points?

A good game is easy to learn but challenging enough to keep you interested.

Creating a Structure

A gameplay designer decides how the game will be structured. It might have different modes for multiple players. There will likely be several different levels. The game has to be fun to play. It needs to be challenging, but not impossible.

If a gameplay designer has an idea that is too hard to program, they may need to think again.

01

COMING TO LIFE

The concept is sketched and the rules are decided. Now it's time to bring the game to life!

Animators take the characters and make them move within the game environment. They use computer programs to create the way a character runs, jumps, and fights. A good animator can show a character's personality in the way they move and react.

There are different software programs to help animate computer games.

Skills

An animator needs to have a talent for drawing characters and movement. They tell stories with moving pictures. They also need to understand how computer games work. They have to design movements that work within the environment and rules of the game.

Animators create a "library" of movements for each character. This way they can re-use them.

Animators might study animals or athletes to learn the different ways that bodies move.

RAMPING IT UP

Gamers love to be thrilled. Adding plenty of effects is one way to do that!

A VFX artist might have to create a digital version of a thunderstorm, with wind and rain.

Visual effects are known as VFX for short. A VFX artist adds the little extras that make a game exciting. They create anything that moves that isn't a character or object. They animate explosions and show dust settling after an impact. Impressive VFX can make a good game great.

Soundtrack

In a computer game, what you hear is just as important as what you see. A sound designer creates a game's soundtrack. This includes music but also sound effects such as crashes, footsteps, or laser blasts. They make sure that the sound matches the visuals.

The sound designer also works with actors who provide voices for the characters.

A composer writes the music for a game. It might be recorded by an orchestra.

TIME TO CODE!

Some jobs in computer games need creativity. Others need programming skills.

When you code, you have to get things just right. Even tiny errors will make the code not work.

Computer games are really just interactive, entertaining computer programs. They have to be coded. That means writing sets of instructions in a language that a computer understands. A gameplay programmer writes the code that makes a game work. They turn the designers' ideas into a fun and exciting game.

The Unity game engine is easy to learn. It can make games for different platforms.

Game Engine

Most computer games are created using a game engine. A game engine is basically a framework. It means that programmers don't have to create everything from scratch. A game engine can render graphics in 2D or 3D. It can add sound and animations.

Unity is one of the most popular game engines. It's free, and even beginners can use it.

01

{ }

MAKING IT WORK

Sometimes the most interesting characters are ones that you don't control.

Artificial intelligence is the ability of a computer to think and learn like a human brain.

Most games have non-playable characters. These characters interact with yours, but you don't control them. An artificial intelligence (AI) programmer writes their code. It controls how these characters behave and make decisions. Their actions must be believable.

It's often important for driving games to look realistic.

Physics in Games

The laws of physics control how objects move in the real world. A physics programmer writes code that decides how objects move within a game. How fast will a rock fall? Will it bounce or smash when it hits the ground? They want it to look realistic.

Physics programmers must be good at math and science as well as coding.

PLAYING TOGETHER

Playing computer games is fun. Playing them with friends is often even better!

Players can play on the same console, or they can play over the internet.

Many games have a multiplayer mode. This means several people can play at once. Their characters are in the same world. They can interact with each other. Sometimes players work together and help each other out. Other times, they are competing against each other to win.

Making Connections

A network programmer writes code so that people can play together. The code lets people in different countries play together online. Network programmers need to understand how computers connect and "talk" to each other.

Some popular games can have thousands of people playing at the same time!

Big online games are stored on servers that your computer connects to.

TEST IT OUT!

A game that doesn't work right can be really annoying. Testing makes sure that doesn't happen.

Some game testers work with gameplay programmers to find fixes for bugs.

Once a game is programmed, testers try it out. Some check that it's fun to play and doesn't get boring. Others look for bugs and technical problems. These might be glitches in the sound or graphics. Testers write reports of each problem, then re-test after it's been fixed.

Testers have to play the same parts of a game over and over.

Playing for Fun?

Being a game tester might sound like a dream job—you get to play computer games all day! However, you're not often playing for fun. You need to have a good eye for detail. You must test all parts of the game without getting distracted.

Game testers look for anything that's wrong, even spelling mistakes in the game's text.

HOW TO PREPARE

If you love computer games then maybe making them is the career for you!

Which part of creating a game interests you the most? If it's designing and drawing new worlds, then maybe you could be a concept artist. If math and science are more your thing, then a physics programmer might be a better role. Whatever your skill is, practice whenever you can.

Playing games is good practice. You'll learn how they operate.

Coding

There's a lot of coding involved in video games. Luckily, it's easy to learn! Try coding your own simple games using a language like Scratch. There are clubs and online classes to show you how to use it. It's never too early to start learning!

Game programmers use many different programming languages. Python, Java, and C++ are popular.

Working with friends is a great way to create, because you can bounce ideas off each other.

QUIZ

Which job in computer games is the best fit for you? Answer these questions, and check your results at the end.

1. What's your favorite after-school activity?

A. soccer–I'm captain of the team

B. meeting with my friends to paint and draw

C. playing video games

2. Which is better, a book or a film?

A. a film, because it takes a team to make one

B. a book, because I like to use my imagination

C. either is great, as long as there are no mistakes that take me out of it

3. What's your strategy when preparing for a test?

A. I make a study schedule and stick to it

B. I always mean to study, but I get distracted by doodling

C. I use flashcards to test myself and review anything that I got wrong

4. How do you clean your room?

A. I come up with a plan for how to clean it and follow the plan.

B. I don't—I prefer to think of it as an exotic alien realm called Messonia.

C. I clean it and then check it to make sure I didn't miss any messy spots.

5. How do you spend your allowance?

A. I always make a budget so I don't run out.

B. I'm saving for a digital pencil to use with my drawing apps.

C. I buy good video games that I can play over and over.

Add up your answers.

What did you get?

Mostly As: You could be a game producer. You like to come up with big ideas, and you're good at leading a team and managing schedules and budgets.

Mostly Bs: You could be a concept artist. You're creative, have a great imagination, and love to draw.

Mostly Cs: You could be a game tester. You love to play computer games, and you have a good eye for detail and spotting mistakes.

GLOSSARY

animator a person who makes moving images, either drawn by hand or created using a computer program

budget a plan setting out how much money is available and how it will be spent

bug an error in a computer program

code a system of letters, numbers, and symbols used as instructions for a computer

composer a person who writes music

console a machine for playing games that is hooked up to a monitor and controllers

digital done electronically

game engine a software framework used to make developing computer games easier and quicker

graphics pictures and other information displayed on a monitor when playing a computer game

mode a particular program or setting in a computer game, such as multiplayer mode

physics the study of forces and the way that they affect objects

platform a particular type of computer hardware or operating system, such as a tablet or gaming console

program a set of coded instructions for a computer to follow

programming language a language that is used to tell computers to do things

server a computer that stores and sends data to other computers

software programs for a computer

3D shown in three dimensions, so that it looks solid and has depth

2D shown in two dimensions, like a flat drawing

virtual reality (VR) a digital environment that is experienced through sights and sounds provided by a computer and in which one's actions partially determine what happens in the environment

FIND OUT MORE

Books

Marquardt, Meg. *Inside Video Games.* North Mankato, MN: Abdo Publishing, 2019.

Schwartz, Heather E. *The History of Gaming.* North Mankato, MN: Capstone Press, 2020.

Wainewright, Max. *Code Your Own Games! 20 Games to Create with Scratch.* New York, NY: Union Square Kids, 2020.

Woodcock, Jon. *Coding Games in Scratch: A Step-by-Step Visual Guide to Building Your Own Computer Games.* New York, NY: DK Children, 2019.

Websites

Here's a brief outline of how video games are made:
wonderopolis.org/wonder/how-are-video-games-made

Learn more about gaming here:
kids.kiddle.co/Video_game

Go here to learn more about coding:
www.dkfindout.com/uk/computer-coding/

This online exhibit tells the history of gaming:
www.pbs.org/kcts/videogamerevolution/history/index.html

Publisher's note to educators and parents: Our editors have carefully reviewed these websites to ensure that they are suitable for students. Many websites change frequently, however, and we cannot guarantee that a site's future contents will continue to meet our high standards of quality and educational value. Be advised that students should be closely supervised whenever they access the internet.

INDEX